ESSA
PRIMAR

Published by:
Lotus Press

ESSAYS FOR PRIMARY CLASSES

Rajeev Bhatia

4735/22, Prakash Deep Building
Ansari Road, Darya Ganj,
New Delhi-110002

Lotus Press : Publishers & Distributors
Unit No. 220, 2nd Floor, 4735/22, Prakash Deep Building,
Ansari Road, Darya Ganj, New Delhi- 110002
Ph.: 32903912, 23280047 • E-mail : lotus_press@sify.com
www.lotuspress.co.in

Essays for Primary Classes
© 2011, Rajeev Bhatia
ISBN: 978-81-8382-243-5
Reprint : 2012

Published by : **Lotus Press,** New Delhi-110002
Printed at : Concept Imprint, Delhi

PREFACE

Essays have become a major part of our formal education. An essay is usually a short piece of writing which is quite often written on various topics and on different levels.

Primary essays play an extremely important role for the child further education. They endeavour the basic information on various topics that varies in our day to day life.

In this book, short essays on various subjects and topics are being highlighted. The main objective of the book is to make the children learn that how to speak or write for yourself. The emphasis is given on children to know how to reproduce new words with their ideas in a relevant manner. Thus will help in enlarging their reading and writing skills also.

Author

CONTENTS

1. MY SCHOOL

I study in Cambridge School which is one of the best school in Delhi. It has a stone building. It has all the facilities a good school should have – well furnished classrooms, laboratories, library and playground. As we enter the school, there is a playground to our left and a small garden to our right. When we enter the building, the Principal's room and office room are to the left, and the staff room is to the right side. There are thirty four class-rooms and all are well furnished.

Our labs are well equipped. Our library has a bulk of books on different subjects. Our Librarian is also very helpful. Our school, like other schools, has a prescribed uniform. We have to wear white or cream cotton shirts, light-blue trousers, black shoes and white socks. Girls have to wear white blouses and light-blue skirts in primary and middle classes and white shirts and light-grey skirts in higher classes. They have to tie a white ribbon also. In our school special attention is paid towards children's behaviour, cleanliness and punctuality, and the most well behaved, neat and punctual student is awarded a prize at the Annual Day function.

Our Principal is a strict disciplinarian. He tries to find out the reason and guides us in many ways. Our teachers are also quite strict. They teach us with great care, check our note-books daily and help us whenever we need them. I like my school very much and I am proud that I belong to a well-reputed school.

2. MY FIRST DAY AT SCHOOL

On the first day my mother accompanied me to school. Other parents also accompanied their children. We all waited in front of the school office.

After a while, a teacher came and led us to some class-rooms and we were put into four separate classes. There some children began to cry as the parents were not allowed into the class-rooms but I did not cry.

It was an enjoyable time for me as I got to know my new classmates. The teacher was very busy writing down our particulars so we had plenty of time to introduce ourselves. Soon recess came. Some of us headed for the bookshop while the rest headed for their parents. I bought a drink with the money my mother had given me. Getting to know my new friends had made me thirsty.

After the recess we went back to our class-room, and my new friends and I managed to coax two boys to stop crying. In fact, soon we were laughing and playing together. Once in a while the teacher had to tell us to keep quiet as we were making too much noise.

Finally, the bell rang for us to go home. Some of us were very relieved to be reunited with our parents. It had been a wonderful first day at school.

3. MY CLASSMATES

In our class Mayank is the noisiest of all boys. His voice is like that of a bull frog, but the volume is louder. In this noisy bunch is a girl who hardly ever opens her mouth and her name is Padma. The boy who sits next to me is such a gentle and soft creature.

Then there is Disha, our class monitor. She sits right in front of the teacher's table. She is such a model student that all the teachers love her. We all love her because she does not boss us around. All she does is to make sure that the teachers have sufficient chalk

to write on the board and that the classroom is clean.

Right at the back of the class sits our
sleepy-head. Manish seems to need more
sleep than others. He catches cat-naps in
between lessons. The funny thing is that
he can fall asleep almost instantly. The
moment the teacher leaves after a lesson,
Manish's snores start up and we know he is
at it again.

Every class has a clown. Our class has
Jimmy. He is always up to some prank or
the other, putting tails on the boys' pants,
frogs in the girls' desks and powdered chalk
on the teacher's chair. So when we hear a
girl scream or see men-teachers strolling
around with chalk on the seat of their pants,
we know that Jimmy has struck again.

The other classmates too have their own
unique personalities. All in all, we are a
group of young children who perhaps are
a bit noisy at times, but on the whole, are
well-behaved and pleasant to be with.

4. PUNISHED IN SCHOOL

One day I was highly shocked when the teacher threw my exercise book at my face. She stood there glowering at me with her huge eyes.

One by one the teacher repeated her nasty actions on a total of five boys. The whole class was dumbfounded by her sudden outburst of anger. We were merely kids and were terrified of her.

Then we were sent to the headmaster's office. The five of us did not know what we had done wrong, but it must be something terrible. Still, we walked bravely into the office.

"You all are troublemakers, aren't you?" the headmaster began. We looked at each other. What trouble did we make?

"I hear you never do what the teacher tells you." We protested but were told to shut up. Gaurav, my classmate, had his hands in his pockets and the headmaster said, "Manners make a man. You've got no manners, boy."

Then the headmaster went on to accuse us of not doing our work properly, being ill-mannered and noisy, among other things. I admit that our work was not top-class material, but the accusations were grossly exaggerated and totally unfounded.

Anyhow, each one of us received a cut of the headmaster's cane. We were punished for flimsy reasons but what could we do? We could do nothing but walk slowly back to class.

5. OUR SCHOOL LIBRARY

Even since I was admitted to this school, I was very keen to see the spacious hall, where only the students of the higher classes were allowed to go during the lunch hour. To others it was something very important, where only one could go with the prior permission of the class-teacher. It was on July 20, that I got a chance of peeping through the glass-panes of big door.

I found out that there were some heavy and some small volumes. These were like toys which even my younger brothers and sisters would like to have. Most of the other books were of an average size and I found that someone was gazing at me.

I could read from the name-plate that he was the librarian. He was having heaps of books on all sides of his table and in shelves. It looked as if he was drowned in a sea of books.

Here I remembered. This library had a Reference Section for teachers also. In all, there were about 6,000 books on various subjects. I was happy that I saw the library that day.

6. PREPARING FOR AN EXAMINATION

The Final Examination is just a couple of months away. It is important that I do well. So I shall have to prepare for it.

First of all, I have to prepare a time-table of study so that I can divide my time properly to the various subjects. I shall have to devote more time to the subjects I am not so good at.

I shall have two study periods a day, one from three to four in the afternoon and the other from seven to nine in the evening. I cannot study all the time because my mind will not be able to cope up with it. So I must have some time to indulge in games and other forms of recreation. Then I can return to my studies with renewed vigour.

In order that I remember the facts I need to do a lot of reading. Only then the facts will remain in my head.

One of the most essential things is that I shall have to cut out time-consuming activities, like socialising with friends, window-shopping, watching videos and listening to pop-songs. I can do these things again once the examinations are over. Meanwhile, it is 'action stations'! There is a battle to be won.

7. THE DAY I WON A PRIZE

I was never a great athlete but once I managed to win a prize. It happened on a School Sports Day when I was asked to represent my class in the Long Jump. My class-master reckoned that I might have a chance to win and he was right.

I did win, but not the first prize. I only managed the second place. We were each given three jumps. There were about ten of us competing for the prizes. When my turn came, I ran down the lane as fast as I could and took off at the board. I thought I jumped very well but it was a foul jump. So I waited for my next jump.

I saw the other competitors leap like gazelles into the sand-pit. One particular boy, the eventual winner, was built like a tank. He was not tall, but his legs were muscular and strong. So when I saw him make his jump, I knew that no one else would be able to beat him.

No one did. I managed my best jump of 3.65 metres and that was nowhere close to his best. The other competitors did much worse.

I was delighted to collect my little plastic prize from the headmaster. It was the first time I had ever won anything. My class-master patted me on my back. I smiled happily as I went home to show the prize to my parents.

8. COMPUTERS TODAY

Computers are referred to in the press, on the radio and television. They appear in films and books and now have invaded all walks of life.

A computer was created for computing fast – a purely mathematical function. Today they are used to forecast the weather, to operate machines, to cut steel to different sizes and even to guide a spacecraft to the moon.

Computers help to trace criminals and are used in the airlines, and the whole world of airlines functions efficiently with its help. Hotels make use of them from managerial capacities to kitchen and companies use them for accounting, invoicing, etc.

Thus, a computer is a data processing device which acts upon data coming to it in all shapes and sizes. It deals with the science of information-processing, invoicing, recording, manipulating, and retrieving information. Computers are electronic devices and all information stored is as patterns of electrical pulses. A computer has to be programmed as per the requirement either to guide a missile or to write poetry. In the years to come, energy-efficient technologies will be at a premium; the micro processor as the key machine will lead the industry. It could easily be concluded that in the long run, "Computerization on a large scale would become essentially a matter of survival."

Hence, it is essential to bring an awareness of computers among the common people.

9. MY FEELINGS ON GETTING LOW MARKS

An examination is at best a gamble but after taking an examination, we know a little what we can expect. There was a sneaking hope in my mind that I might get a merit position.

On the day the results were to come, I reached school before time. As soon as the results were put on the board, I hunted for my roll number. I had secured a first division but just scraped through it. I could not believe it. How could I get such low marks?

All my answers were correct. Then how I had scored only 80% marks in Mathematics? And how the hell I could get barely 45 marks in Social Studies? I was very good in it. I felt cheated.

At first I felt like crying. In desperation I could have committed suicide. All my hard work had gone waste! What did they mean by giving me such low marks? I deserved better. They probably evaluated my papers after a quarrel or in a bad mood. But why should I be made to suffer?

I felt shy of facing my friends and teachers. Gradually, anger and shame gave way to a dull acceptance of my fate. My parents comforted me by telling that there are other examinations, too. Moreover, a first division is not so bad that I should feel so miserable. What cannot be cured must be endured. Anyway, time is a great healer. I listened to them and kept quiet.

10. MY CLASS MONITOR

My name is Neha. I study in 3rd standard. There are forty students in our class. Among all Sheena is the most intelligent girl and is the monitor of our class. She is eight years old. She is a well behaved girl among all and so controls the class very well. Our teacher says she is a very responsible girl and always does her work well.

Sheena is my best friend. Our teachers have a blind faith in her and had assigned her for the daily assignments. After every class she gives us our daily assignment and checks our homework the next day. Every student feels very proud of her as she never lies to anyone. She cleans the blackboard every day before the teacher's arrival and looks for the fine chalk and duster being placed on the table.

Once in a week we organise a conversation class. In it we learn and practice to speak English willingly.

She is very helpful to the classmates and fair in decision. Last time in the terminal examination she scored first in the class. She is very good in studies and always helps us in our difficulties. We take turns in becoming the class monitors but everyone knows that Sheena is the best!

11. THE RESPONSIBILITIES OF AN IDEAL STUDENT

A student can never be educated until and unless he does not put his heart and soul to the cause of education. A student is a person who devotes himself to the pursuits of knowledge and learning. The pursuit of knowledge demands hard work and full devotion. Unfortunately, the students do not realise their duties.

In practical life, only those students come out with best colours, who have acquired maximum knowledge.

An ideal student enjoys learning. He goes deeper and deeper in search of the knowledge. He is not a bookworm. He knows that a healthy body is necessary for a healthy mind. He takes interest in all the activities that promote his physical health. He goes to the playground with the same pleasure and enthusiasm with which he studies in the library. An ideal student is not unsocial. He loves his fellow students and participates in all the collective activities.

The ideal student respects and honours his teachers. He knows the place of teachers who are opening the gate of glories for him. He is humble and obedient. The more he learns from his teachers, the more grateful he is to them. The more knowledge he gets, the more humble he becomes. He is always regular and punctual. He does not participate in adverse and negative activities. He confines himself to his studies and tasks. He does not waste his time in useless deeds. He is kind and generous.

12. TEACHERS, GOOD AND BAD

Having been in school for a number of years now, I have come across many types of teachers. Some are good while some are bad.

The good ones are those who put effort into their work to make the students knowledgeable and thus care for the welfare of their students. They genuinely want to teach us what they know. So despite their weaknesses we love and respect them.

Our present class teacher, Mr. Saxena, is a model teacher. He not only teaches us

English, but more importantly, he is a great human being. He is invariably patient, very approachable and always has a practical solution to any problem anyone may present to him. We are grateful for his guidance and advice.

On the other hand, our Mathematics teacher is the worst of the lot. Normally, he just sits at the table and tells us to do exercise this or that. Sometimes he does not come at all. Rarely does he teach. When he does, it is almost impossible to follow him. His hands tremble and his speech is incoherent. So, we are left to our own devices. Fortunately for me, Mathematics is not too difficult. So I can cope even without a teacher.

In between these two are the other teachers. Some are good in some ways and bad in others. However, all of them are predictable. So, we know what to do when in their presence. The good ones we appreciate and respect. The bad ones we tolerate.

13. WAYS OF IMPROVING MY ENGLISH

Today, English is used widely. It has become the most popular language of communication between countries and in many fields of human endeavour. So it is important that we must learn to use English, otherwise, we will be at a disadvantage.

The only effective way of improving my English is to use it as often as possible.

In school we communicate in English during our English classes. But it is not enough. So wherever possible I speak English with some of my friends and teachers who can speak or communicate with me in English.

Reading books, magazines and newspapers are good ways of improving English. On the whole, they are grammatically correct. We may speak incorrect English and get away with it, but not so with printed words they have to be correct. Through reading, I learned how to use correct English in writing and speaking, though at times I still speak the broken English that many of us speak in our day-to-day life.

Watching television and listening to the radio are two more ways of improving my English. English as a language spoken by the Britishers, Americans, Australians and others in distinctly different.

So I continue to use English that is understandable to hear, read, speak and write. Some of my friends only hear and read it. They can hardly speak or write it, but I will not be like them. I will try my best to master it.

14. A PAINFUL LESSON

Our bodies are made of flesh and bones. Any time any part is injured and we feel pain. So we must try to avoid injury as much as we can. Usually it takes a painful lesson to teach us to avoid injury. The following was a particularly painful one.

I, like any young child, love to run around as quickly as I can. It is fun. However, there is danger of falling down which can result in painful injuries.

One day while playing "catching" with some friends, I happened to run down a hill. I found that running down a hill was easy and I could go very fast. At the spur of the moment I decided to see how fast I could go, so I ran with all my might.

Alas, I ran too fast for my legs to keep up. One moment I was running, the next I fell sprawling onto the tarmac road. The shock was horrible as I scraped along the hard surface of the road.

The pain was intense as I lay on the road writhing. My hands, legs and face were bleeding from where my skin had been scraped off. When my friends came to help me, they were horrified to see me in such a bloody mess.

Anyhow, they summoned help and I was taken to the hospital. There they cleaned and dressed my wounds. All the time I felt as though I was on fire.

I suffered for two weeks, thereafter, every time they changed the bandages, it was terrible.

I learned my lesson. It is foolish to run down a hill.

15. A FRIGHTFUL EXPERIENCE

Once I had to walk through an area filled with undergrowth to get to the shop. It was not too unpleasant except that I had to keep to the narrow footpath and not blunder into the bushes.

Buying some flour from the shop seemed harmless enough. The shop was the nearest one and my mother reckoned, I was old enough to run a simple errand for her.

Suddenly, I heard a growl from within some bushes. A ferocious dog appeared in front of me with its fangs bared and I froze.

If the dog were to attack me I knew I could not fight with him.

I had heard that if you keep still, a dog would not attack. It worked. The dog came up to me and sniffed me all over, but he did not bite me. I trembled with fear but dared not to move.

After a while he lay down beside me. I thought it was safe to go, but the moment I moved a leg he stood up and growled fiercely again. I was trapped! The dog would not let me move. What could I do?

I waited in fear. As long as I remained still, I was all right, but how long could I stand there like that? My feet were already feeling numb.

Then I had an idea. The shop was just a short distance away. I shouted "Help! Help!" with all my might. The dog looked confused but did not attack me.

The shopkeeper heard my shouts and came to investigate. The dog, which was obviously his, wagged his tail and folded back his ears. He quickly brought a chain and tied him to a post. I was so relieved. The shopkeeper apologised and gave me a free packet of flour.

What a frightful experience it was! Anyway, I never had any more trouble with the dog. The shopkeeper kept him tied up thereafter.

16. LUNCH BREAK

Our school is a day school. Its working hours are from 10.10 a.m. to 4.30 p.m. We have four periods in the morning and four in the afternoon. There is a 30 minute break at 1.10 a.m. This is lunch hour for both teachers and students. It is also play and gossip time for students. Towards the end of the fourth period itself, students become restive. Their attention is more on the watch than what the teacher is trying to teach. They eagerly wait for the bell.

As soon as the recess bell goes, the calm of the school is broken. There is noise everywhere. Some students rush down the stairs pushing each other to reach the canteen. Others could be seen sitting in the classroom and gobbling up their food. The younger ones could be seen roaming about eating their lunch.

Soon there is great rush at the taps. Many students straightaway rush to the playground. Others join them after finishing their lunch. The playground gets crowded and there is hardly any game possible. Yet students manage to play. Library is also filled to capacity during lunch hour. Many students could be seen browsing through the papers and magazines.

Soon the time is over. The bell goes. Children rush to their classes and the school becomes quiet again. Recess is the best part of the school day. Students and teachers all enjoy it.

17. MY CHILDHOOD

All children like places which can give them fun. They all like playing in the park, on the beach, and in the zoo, with lots of friends. Some of them are lucky because their parent spends time with them, but some of them are not. I think I belong to the lucky side. When I was a child, my parents always spent time playing with me. I remembered a lot of places where I spent valuable time with them. My favourite childhood places were zoo and park.

Winter is the best time to visit a zoo and we usually have a visit. When I was a child, my parents didn't allow me to feed big animals. They gave me a lot of good memories. We usually bought some food like bread, cookies, and bananas. It took twenty minutes to walk to there, and from park to zoo you just have to cross the main road. There were a lot of animals, like birds, monkeys, deer, foxes, and tigers. Several times my parents took my friends and me to visit there. We tore food into small pieces and threw it to them. Even though I wasn't tall enough to catch balls, I still enjoyed the every moment. The grass was very soft and the sky was very clear. Thus, being a child is great fun!

18. DANGER AT HOME

Our home is usually our favourite place where we love to spend maximum time. However, many accidents occur at home. There are many dangerous things in the house and we should be aware of them. Thus, we can avoid unnecessary pain or injury.

Electricity runs many of our home appliances. It is a very useful thing. It is also a very dangerous thing and if used carelessly, it can harm us. Electrical sockets and power points are to be handled with utmost care.

Kids should never be allowed to go near them. Unless we are very sure of what we are doing, repairs should only be done by a competent electrician. It is only too easy to get electrocuted. Old or faulty appliances should be discarded. If used, they are likely to start a fire somewhere or kill someone who touches it carelessly.

The kitchen has many dangerous things. Sharp knives can draw blood, mishandled gas-cylinders can explode, hot water can scald and stoves can cause nasty burns. Flies and rats can contaminate food. Thus we should be very careful while working in a kitchen. If we are careful and know how to handle these things, then the chance of an accident occurring is lessened.

The biggest danger in a bathroom is when the floor is slippery with water or soap. I have heard of many incidents of people, especially old folk, falling in the bathroom. Sometimes the fall is fatal. Often it leaves the victim bedridden. Utmost care is needed here.

Finally, the medicine cabinet should be inaccessible to young children. Dangerous drugs and pills can look like sweets to these young ones. If taken, the consequences can be disastrous.

Other dangers also exist. It is up to us to watch out for them.

19. A BIRTHDAY PARTY

Reema is my neighbour. She turned twelve recently and her parents held a birthday party for her and I was invited to the party.

The party began at about three in the afternoon. There were about twenty of us children gathered in Reema's house. We all were dressed in our best clothes. Everyone, especially Reema, was wearing a pretty dress and was looking the most beautiful with a smile on her face.

We gave several gifts to Reema and she

happily opened them. It must really be exciting to receive all those gifts.

After that Reema's mother served us soft drinks and delicious tid-bits. We then played some games like "Musical Chairs" and "Treasure Hunt". The winners were given prizes.

At about four-thirty her mother brought out the birthday cake. It was beautifully decorated with pink and white icing. Twelve colourful candles were set in the middle of the cake. We all sang "Happy Birthday to Reema" after which she blew out the candles and cut the cake. We clapped our hands eagerly.

We helped ourselves to slices of the delicious cake and after that we continued with our games.

Finally, at about six in the evening the party came to an end. We were all tired but happy. The parents of the other children came to collect them. I helped Reema and her mother clean up the mess we had made. After that I walked home which was only two doors away.

20. THINGS I LIKE TO DO

I like playing the guitar. Though I am not very good at it, but I am learning and can play some tunes. I spend a lot of time playing the guitar that sometimes I get scolded by my mother. I suppose I tend to spend a bit too much time with it. Anyhow, playing the guitar is very enjoyable.

I also like taking evening walks around my neighbourhood. In the evening the air is cool and refreshing. The children are busy playing and the neighbours are friendlier. So I take leisurely strolls, sometimes stopping to play with other children and sometimes stopping to chat with the neighbours.

Another thing that I like doing is getting up late in the morning. During weekdays I have to get up early or I will be late for the school. On Saturdays, Sundays and holidays, it is so pleasurable to just lie on bed till late in the morning without having to get up and hurry for school. Again I tend to lie too long in bed and my mother has to come and scold me to get up.

Listening to the radio and watching television are also things I like to do. Of course, I do not listen and watch everything. I only tune in to my favourite programmes and enjoy myself while seated on my favourite chair.

There are other things that I enjoy doing, too, but there seems to be not enough time to do them all. So I generally just stick to doing those I mentioned, plus any others that I have time for.

21. HOW I SPENT THE WEEKEND

Nothing extraordinary happened last weekend. It was just like any other ordinary weekend.

I got up later than usual on Saturday morning. After breakfast I went to my friend Arun's house and spent some time there by reading comics. Arun has tons of comics. His father buys the latest for him. Being his friend, I get to read them, too.

We read comics till lunch-time. Then I went home, had lunch and took an afternoon nap. Taking an afternoon nap is a pleasure that I can indulge only on weekends. On weekdays I do not have time for it.

The rest of the afternoon I helped my father in the garden uprooting weeds and trimming the hedge. We continued until darkness fell. After that I had my bath and dinner. After dinner I watched the television until it was time for bed.

On Sunday morning, too, I got up late. For breakfast I had cornflakes with milk while watching T.V. Then I spent the rest of the morning doing my homework.

Again I took a nap after lunch. Then I finished up my homework. By the time I was done with the homework, it was already evening. So I took a stroll around the neighbourhood. It was a great feeling to be able to relax after all the homework had been done. After dinner, I packed my books in my bag and went to bed early. I had to get enough sleep, otherwise I would fall asleep in school the next day.

22. GRANDMA

My Grandma is too old. Her hairs are snowy-white; skin wrinkled and teeth all gone. She is also quite deaf. The doctor said she is senile.

So she always forgets where she has kept things and will often frantically search for them. Again, she forgets what she is searching for, which adds to her frustration. When she misplaces her spectacles, she will have someone else's pair and happily go about the house. She cannot remember whether she just had dinner, but can remember an event that happened fifty years ago. Sometimes her deafness troubles her a lot. She says we are scolding her.

In between bouts of crankiness, she sometimes seems normal. But this seems to get lesser as her disease progresses. So we do our best to keep her out of the harmful way. We lock the medicine cabinet and doors and hide dangerous things from her. It would be disastrous if she swallowed a bottle of pills or got lost while wandering in the streets. The latter has happened before and a kind neighbour brought her back to home.

It is unfortunate that the last years of her life have to be like this, but it is so. We can do nothing but to help her along as much as we can.

23. POWER FAILURE

One evening, when I was getting ready to watch a cartoon show on television, there was a power failure. The television set just went blank, the lights went off and the fan slowed down and stopped. As it was getting dark, I hoped that the power would be restored soon but it was not to be so.

Soon darkness enveloped the neighbourhood. We hastily lit candles so that we could find our way around the house. As we had only three candles, my mother sent me to the sundry shop nearby to buy more candles.

"Sorry, no candles," said the shopkeeper. The neighbours had bought up all the candles. At home my father managed to dig out two kerosene lamps. We lit these, too, and kept the darkness out.

The fan was not running and it was oppressively warm. Furthermore, there was nothing to do but wait for the power to come on again. All of us sat quietly in the living-room. We had grown so dependent on electricity. Without it we felt so uncomfortable. I used a book to fan myself.

Finally, it was time for bed and still there was no power. Nevertheless, I groped my way to my room, changed and lay quietly in the darkness. It felt so strange without the familiar lights around me. Anyhow, I fell asleep after a while.

The power came back only at dawn. By then we did not need it anymore.

24. PESTS IN THE HOME

We seem quite unaware of their presence and do not seem to know that they have been bitten. Well, these are lucky people until they come down with malaria or dengue fever.

Another persistent pest is the common rat. These animals are very active during the night, looking for food everywhere. They eat anything, even soap. So any food left uncovered overnight is likely to be contaminated by these pests. Furthermore, rats make nests in nooks and corners of the house. They nibble into floorboards, ceilings and even electrical wiring. They are really a big nuisance.

Cockroaches too are pests. They have the habit of crawling all over the place. Sometimes they even crawl onto one's body. These dirty little creatures contaminate food, too. They also emit a strong stench. It is never pleasant to encounter them.

25. MY NEIGHBOURS

Many of us live in housing apartments. I live in one of the aparements independently. The one thing about living in a housing apartment is that we have many neighbours.

Next to my house on the right lives a family whose parents seem to be always scolding the children. Never a day passes without hearing the children crying and the parents shouting at the top of their voices.

On the other side of my house, however, lives a very quiet and polite family. Though they have four children, which is one more than the other family, I never hear them scolding their children.

Further down the road is a family whose radio is switched on most of the time, except late at night. Then there is a family whose members seem to live in a world of their own. They are not blind and neither deaf. I guess they are simply not interested in knowing their neighbours.

On the opposite side of the road live Mr. Lamba and his family. Mr. Lamba is a bird-collector. So, every day a dozen or more birds sing melodious tunes right beneath his front porch. However, the bird droppings can give off an awful stench.

These are some of the neighbours living close to my house. The friendly ones smile or raise their hands while the unfriendly ones keep away.

26. A NIGHTMARE

Don't eat just before going to bed!" my mother used to tell me. "You might get a nightmare." I never believed her until it happened to me.

One late night, I felt very hungry. So I made myself a peanut-butter sandwich and a large cold glass of milk. After consuming them I went to bed.

Soon I drifted off into a troubled sleep. I dreamt that I was with a group of people looking for an old woman. I was not sure why we were looking for her but we all seemed very afraid of her. I was searching high and low for her in frightful places I had never been before. Sometimes I seemed to be flying while at other times I seemed unable to move.

After some searching I entered a darkened room and saw a figure sleeping on a bed. As I got nearer, the figure suddenly threw away the blanket, got up and stared at me. It was an ugly old woman with shiny golden teeth. She raised her claw-like fingers and walked towards me. I wanted to run but was unable to hide.

The next moment I gave a muffled yell and found myself panting on my bed. My goodness, what a horrible nightmare it was! For a minute or so I lay on my bed not daring to close my eyes for fear of falling asleep again and continuing the nightmare. Then I sat on my bed until the horrible feeling got washed through my mind. From then onwards. I never eat just before going to sleep.

27. MY HOBBY

My hobby is reading. I read story books, magazines, newspapers and any kind of material that I find interesting.

This hobby got started when I was a little boy. I always wanted my parents to read fairy tales and other stories to me. Soon they got fed up and tired of reading the stories for me. I started with simple ABC books. Soon I could read simple fairy tales and other stories.

Reading enables me to learn about so many things that I would otherwise never come to know. I learned about the wonders of the world, space travel, human achievements, gigantic whales, tiny viruses and other fascinating things of our world.

The wonderful thing about reading is that I do not have to learn things the hard way. For example, I do not have to catch a disease to know that it can kill me. I know the danger so I can avoid it.

Books provide the reader with so much information and facts. They have certainly helped me in my daily life. I am better equipped to cope with living. Otherwise, I would go about ignorantly learning things the hard way.

28. FIVE THINGS I LIKE

All of us have our likes and dislikes. So have I, and my dislikes are many. But out of my likes I have five on the top. These are poetry, music, excursions, meeting people and reading thought-provoking books and magazines.

Being a student of literature, I have read Wordsworth and his poems have left their lasting effect on me. Other poets of nature who have impressed me the most are Keats, Tagore, Robinson. Many people say, music has its effect even on trees, plants, animals and their growth.

Milch cows have shown better yield of milk due to music. I like Michael Jackson the most. I have gone on excursions to almost all nearby hill stations and health resorts. I prefer to go on educational, scientific and historical tours also. Meeting people from various professions is another hobby.

I have pen-friends among intellectuals, artists, and actors, dancers, scientists and university professors. Reading books on philosophy, religion, anthropology, world history and literature is my last liking. I subscribe to magazines and read books on these subjects.

29. MY LAST SUNDAY

Sundays generally have a fixed routine for the TV programmes. But my last Sunday was quite different. On Monday I had two papers – English and Mathematics. Due to unavoidable circumstances, I had not been able to do any revision. So, I had planned to get up early and had set the alarm clock to wake me up, but I got up very late. I had to skip through my lessons in English to make up for the lost time.

After breakfast, I started revising Maths and got stuck in the third problem. I was still trying to solve it when my uncle came with his family. I had to go to the market. When I returned, I learnt that the maid had not come and I had to help in laying the table and doing odd jobs.

I was free only when they left at 5 p.m. I went to my room and bolted the door, so that I could study undisturbed. By the time I really settled down there was a breakdown of electricity. Mother advised me to go to sleep and promised to wake me up as soon as the electricity came. As there was no current till late at night, we all went to sleep.

When I got up, it was almost 5 o'clock. The lights were on in all the rooms. I became worried and went round to see what was the matter. I found everyone in sound sleep. I tried to sit and study but I was so angry and anxious that I could not concentrate. Anyway, now it was time to get up and get ready. Thus, the whole of the last Sunday was wasted. I could neither watch TV and enjoy, nor could study.

30. A RAINY DAY

This year the summer season was unduly long and extremely hot. Going to the school, studying in the class or playing on the ground, all seemed to be a punishment.

One morning, clouds gathered in the sky. There were vivid flashes of lightning and it started raining. There was a downpour for a while, but soon it turned into steady raining. It was time for school. So, we carried our umbrellas and set out. It was refreshing to go out in the cool air.

The sound of falling rain was pleasing to the ears. Buses were late and overcrowded. It may be quite pleasant to take a brisk walk in the rain; nobody likes standing in the queue in wet clothes with the drops from other persons' umbrellas dropping down the back with cold clammy frequency.

The street urchins were having a great time playing in the streets, floating boats on the sides of the roads where water was flowing fast. In the class, very few students were attentive. Almost everybody was looking out and watching rain every now and then.

Our school gate and the road had ankle-deep water. The municipality had been caught napping. The drainage system was choked. All low lying areas had knee-deep water. It is exhilarating to watch pouring rain and to run about in it, but soon I was happy to return back home and immediately changed my wet clothes.

31. NEWSPAPERS

Life without newspaper is difficult to imagine. It is the first thing that we look for every morning. It brings us news and views from all corners of the world. Any event or occurrence of importance that takes place is reported by the newspapers.

The newspapers carry information for everyone – businessman, politician, unemployed people, players and kids, etc. It widens knowledge, keeps one abreast of all advances made in the fields of science, education, medicine and technology.

Newspapers are important pillars in a democracy. A free press not only makes people aware of the views and policies of the government, but also of their rights.

It keeps the government informed about people's wishes, desires and aspirations, which can be expressed. Newspaper keep us in constant touch with the news, developments, changes, advances and occurrences in each nook and corner of the world and at a very little price to the reader. Their popularity give them immense power in moulding public opinion.

Unfortunately, most newspapers have vested interests. They are owned by capitalists and have to toe their line. Some newspapers are organs of political parties. Their loyalty to the party is greater than the sense of fairplay. It is essential to cultivate the faculty of independent thinking in the readers, so that they do not believe every word of the news. The newspaper should have a very strict code of ethics to which it should conscientiously adhere.

32. MY HOME

The saying 'East or West, home is the best' is true in many ways. Home offers affection and security. My home to me is the best place in the world, where I live with my mother, father, a brother and a sister.

I belong to a middle class family. My home is a cozy little flat on the 1st floor in Dwarka. Our drawing-cum-dining room is tastefully decorated. It has a TV set, a sofa, a refrigerator and a dining table. The decoration pieces remind me of our visits to different places. There are two bedrooms.

One is used by my parents and the other is shared by three of us. Not only the room but the study-table is also shared by us.

Ours is a small and happy family, where every member has consideration for the needs and comforts of each other. We all share household work, too. Our mornings are usually busy as all are in a great hurry to complete their work. But either it's breakfast, lunch or dinner time, we all have it together. At that moment we share all that we had enjoyed or suffered during the day.

We always keep our home clean and tidy. Everything is kept in its proper place. I like my home, very much.

33. AN ACCIDENT

The road in front of my school is a narrow one and is always full of rush. Every afternoon when school is dismissed, the road becomes almost impassable as children, bicycles, cars and buses jostle and struggle to use it. Sometimes a policeman is there to help things out, but generally, chaos reigns and we have to be careful not to get involved in an accident. A few accidents have already occurred and I am a witness to one.

It happened just after the school. As usual the road was very busy and the vehicles were running in a great hurry. There was a loud blare of horn, a squeal of brakes and I saw a car knock into a boy. He fell as though his feet were swept under him.

Fortunately, the car was not moving very fast and the driver managed to stop the car before a wheel could run over the fallen boy.

Suddenly, all the traffic stopped. I ran over to the boy and saw blood on the road. He was bleeding from a cut on his head. A man came and carried him to a hospital. A policeman came to calm things down.

As there was nothing I could do, I turned and walked down the road carefully. It was terrible to witness an accident. I certainly would not like to be involved in one.

34. AN AUTOBIOGRAPHY OF A MOTORCYCLE

I was made in a factory in Haryana. I was one of 100 c.c. motorcycles that were sent down to Kuala Lumpur to be sold. So I found myself waiting patiently in a shop for someone to buy me.

A few weeks later, a man came and bought me for his son. The boy was barely seventeen but his father was rich and could afford to buy me. I was chosen mainly because of my beautiful red colour and that I could go quite fast.

My young owner was a reckless rider. He rode me carelessly all over the town, every time putting me in danger. Many times I thought for sure that it was the end but somehow he managed to escape.

However, he tried different tricks carelessly. One fateful day my owner took me out on a reckless ride and was in such a hurry that he overtook every overcoming vehicle. After a few near misses, he finally made a mistake and he slammed head-first into the back of a lorry. I slid uncontrollably under the lorry. That was the end of him.

I was salvaged from under the lorry, repaired and sold again to a middle-aged man who delivered newspapers for a living. So for the next five years I was made to run thousands of kilometres carrying loads of newspapers.

The hard work took its toll on me, and despite several repairs, my owner decided that it was time to retire me. I was too worn-out to be of any use anymore. So I was sold to a motorcycle shop where the owner stripped me of my parts.

Today, I am nothing but a bare frame without any wheels. I await the day when I will be sold for scrap. That would be the end of mine.

35. CHILDREN'S DAY

Children's day is celebrated in India on 14th November every year with great celebrations. It is celebrated on the birthday of Pt. Jawaharlal Nehru who loved children and was loved by them and who called him as 'Chacha Nehru.'

Children's Day is an event celebrated on various days in many places around the world. International Children's Day is celebrated on June 1 and Universal Children's Day is on November 20. Other countries celebrate a local 'Children's Day' on other dates.

The reason why Nehru's birthday has been chosen for the celebration of children is because of his love and passion for children. Pandit Nehru is also regarded as the country's Special Child, to have been the first Prime Minister, after his long struggle for independence.

The day is marked with a lot of activities for children. But the fact remains that only a section of the country's children actually have an opportunity to celebrate their existence. Schools organise events and activities that their students thoroughly enjoy, but there is an entire population of young ones that are left ignored on this special day – the downtrodden street children.

36. STREET-FIGHT

People have become so volatile, they have so little tolerance that even a trifle is enough to ignite their temper. Street-fights are becoming more and more frequent now adays.

Once I witnessed such a fight from close quarters. When I was returning from my school, I saw two boys quarrelling for a ball. But before I reached there, two ladies came out from the adjoining houses to find out why their children were crying. Instead of separating the kids, surprisingly, they started quarrelling among themselves. A slanging match started. Voice were raised on both sides. Soon many ladies came out of their houses and surrounded them. None tried to stop them. Some even added fuel to the fire by their comments. It seemed as if they had used up all their abusive vocabulary and were about to come to blows. One had already started tearing the hair of the other. Then my grandmother came out.

She is somewhat hard of hearing. But even she had heard their voices. She in her forthright manner scolded both and silenced them, and enquired about the reason. To everyone's surprise they both told her that the son of the other one had taken her son's ball, and was quarrelling with him. I could not help laughing when I saw that both the boys were playing happily with that ball a few minutes later.

37. TURNING OVER A NEW LEAF

Rohit was the naughtiest boy in our class. In fact I would say that he was the naughtiest in the whole school. He always seemed to get in trouble with the prefects and teachers. The prefects avoided him and the teachers had a hard time while controlling him.

He was destructive, to say the least. Our classroom did not have a single window pane as he had broken all of them. Over in a corner lay a heap of broken desks and chairs, the result of his handiwork. He had been caned twice in front of the whole school for his misdeeds but he remained unrepentant. I was sure that he would be sacked from school if he carried his behaviour in the same manner.

One day Rohit's mother died. For a whole week he was absent from school. When he returned, he was totally changed. I nearly did not recognize him. For a moment I thought we had a new classmate, but it was Rohit well-groomed and neatly dressed.

Not only his appearance changed but his behaviour also changed dramatically. He had become the most well-behaved boy in the class. No longer did he break chairs or anything else. The teachers and prefects were visibly shocked, but they were glad for it.

It was a miracle that Rohit turned over a new leaf. One day he confided to me that it was his mother's death that changed him. He realised how horrible he had been just before his mother died. So he made a promise to his mother at her deathbed to change himself into a well behaved boy and thus he kept his promise.

I am glad for him. He is now a pleasure to be with and one of my best friends.

38. THE WAY WE EAT

The way we eat our food is habitual. This means that we are usually not aware of it. I have noticed some of the ways people eat and they range from elegance to gluttony.

My father slurps his soup. It is disgusting but we never dare to say anything and will be sorely offended if we did. On the other hand, my mother is so graceful in her ways. It is a pleasure to watch her daintily scoop the food up into her mouth and then chew it slowly and gently.

A fat friend of mine literally gobbles up his food. He eats at least three times as much as I do and in about half the time that I take. While he is eating, he is totally oblivious to his surroundings. He puts the food into his mouth as fast as he can, chews a couple of times and then swallows it. It does not matter whether he is using a spoon, chopsticks or his hands. He is skilled with all. After finishing he sits up, gives a couple of burps and rubs his belly. It is all very disgusting, but at the same time, it is very amusing.

Another friend of mine, a thin one this time, hardly eats at all. He sits at the table and half-heartedly picks up the food with a fork. He says he has no appetite. No wonder he is so thin.

Then there are many who talk while they eat. So, little pieces of food and drops of saliva start flying. Only a sharp "Shut up and eat!" can silence these talkers. They usually shut up but only for a while.

How do you eat your food? Do you eat quickly, slowly, like a glutton, sparingly, daintily or noisily? Do you lick your fingers, spoon or plate? Are you aware of how you eat?

39. CONFINED TO THE HOUSE

It all began with a blister on my lower eyelid. I happened to rub it accidentally and it was painful.

Soon after blisters appeared on my hands and neck. I suspected that I must be coming down with something. My mother examined me and immediately pronounced "chicken-pox". I had come down with chicken-pox.

She took me to the doctor to make sure. The doctor said that what I needed was proper rest. He gave me a two-week medical certificate and some pills to keep down the fever. Two weeks! I had to stay in the house for two weeks.

Very quickly more blisters appeared all over my body. I even had some in the throat, which made swallowing difficult. To make matters worse, I began to get bouts of fever. At times when the fever was raging, I seemed to drift into a kind of limbo. Things became hazy and I was not sure whether I was awake or dreaming.

I had a look in the mirror and saw that my face was grotesque. Red blisters covered my whole face. I wondered if I would be scarred permanently.

So I stayed in the house and did nothing. It was not too unpleasant except for the fever and the extra care I had to take not to break the blisters accidentally. Nobody came to visit me. I was forbidden to visit others. It was customary to remain out of sight when one had chicken-pox. I had no choice but to comply.

The days passed. Slowly the blisters dried into dark scabs which flaked off after a while, leaving behind little red scars. The flakes fell on the floor, on the bed and on my clothes.

For two weeks I remained confined to the house. At the end of the period, my appearance had improved enough for me to go back to school. The little scars remained there for a few more months, but I was glad my enforced stay in the house was over.

40. THE GARBAGE COLLECTORS

It is incredible how much rubbish we throw into the garbage bin. It always seems to be full. The smell can be quite strong. So we are very thankful to the garbage collectors who come and remove the garbage.

They normally come thrice a week. If they miss a day or two, then the garbage bins in my neighbourhood overflow onto the road. This invites stray dogs and other scavengers. Only when the garbage truck comes again, is the problem taken care of.

So we can see how important these garbage collectors are.

When they come, they usually make a lot of noise. Often they are moody. We bear them because they are not doing a pleasant job. It is dirty and smelly. Perhaps they are used to it. Nevertheless, they do come regularly to perform an important job. On festive occasions we give them gifts, usually small amounts of money as a token of appreciation for a job well done. Granted, they are noisy, dirty and sometimes cranky, but how else can they behave when they have to do work that most people would not touch? Nobody would like to work as a garbage collector.

Anyhow, someone has to do the dirty job. The least we can do is to make their job easier by keeping our garbage in proper bins and showing them a little appreciation now and then.

41. THE MAD WOMAN

I went for a walk every morning. Sometimes I come across a mad woman dressed in a dark dirty sari. She probably has not taken a bath. Her hair is matted, teeth stained red with betel-nut and eyes blood-shot with the look of madness.

It is never pleasant when I see her standing by the roadside. She is by no means violent but has the nasty habit of following people who pass by her side. Normally, when I see her, I cross over the other side of the road just to avoid her. Usually that works. Sometimes she crosses the road, too. So I have to run.

Fortunately, she cannot run very fast and gives up after a while.

One morning, as I crossed the road to avoid her, she tried to cross, too. I started to run. She started running, too, but tripped on her sari. She fell down hard on the road and lay there in a heap. I wanted to keep running, but I saw that she was in great danger of being run over by a car. So I ran back and pulled her to the roadside.

It's true that I disliked it but I had to help her. The other passers-by did not seem to bother. So I held my breath and pulled her by her arms towards the roadside. By now people and cars had stopped watching. No one helped, but at last I managed to drag her to safety.

She opened her eyes and gave me a smile. I could only stare at her dumbly. Then I turned and hurried to school to wash my hands.

I am going to get a bicycle to have a pedal drive to my school. It is much faster this way. Also I will not have to contend with the mad woman again.

42. A CLOSE BRUSH WITH DEATH

It was raining heavily the last night. Fortunately, we were in a car and my uncle, who was driving, had the situation under control.

We passed slowly by an oil-palm estate. The driving rain made visibility poor. So my uncle drove very carefully. He had all the lights on of the car. So did the other drivers. I could make out little blobs of light on the other cars through the white sheet of rain.

Overhead, black clouds hovered ominously. It felt as though they were about to fall on us at any moment. Lightning streaked across the sky and onto the distant hills. The ensuing thunder rumbled unceasingly. Some flashes of lightning came uncomfortably close and the resulting thunderclap was deafening, even with all our windows up.

All of a sudden a bright flash of light blinded us and a very loud crack made me lose my bearings. The next thing I knew was that my uncle had stopped the car and his face was pale with shock. I too was in shock. What had happened?

For a long agonising moment I struggled to collect my scattered wits. Then my uncle pointed a trembling finger at something outside the car. I looked in the direction and saw an oil-palm some ten metres away literally split in half through the middle. It was scorched black and smoking. I then realised that it had just been struck by lightning.

If the lightning had struck us instead, we would be scorched black and smoking, too. Still trembling, my uncle quickly drove away from the danger zone. We had just had a close brush with death. It was close, too close for comfort.

43. SOME FUNNY PEOPLE I HAVE MET

The first funny person that comes to my mind is a man who sits on the branch of a tree by a road and shouts at the car that passes by. He is mad of course, but still it is strange that a madman can shout at passing cars. He never seems to notice me somehow when I pass by on my bicycle. For him it is only cars. He shouts with such gusto and pleasure. I always laugh when I see him shouting.

Then there is a man in baggy shorts and Japanese slippers who rides his motorcycle with only the right side of his buttocks on the seat and the left side hanging out. This makes his motorcycle lean at an awkward angle as though he is about to fall, but he does not. Perhaps he has a large boil on the left side of his buttocks. Whatever the reason, I have seen him riding the way he does many times. He looks so funny, and dangerous.

Running a sundry shop near my house is a short and stout man whose body-shape and movements resemble that of a penguin. I do not mean to be derogatory, but he always reminds me of that bird. However, he runs his shop well and I get lots of things from there.

Finally, there is a dandy who dresses in the most outrageous outfits I have ever seen. The colour combination he chooses for his clothes are, to say the least, horrible. Only he dares to wear a purple shirt with green trousers and a pink tie. Often I see him running around on his motorcycle wearing those loud clothes. He works as a salesman for some company. Perhaps those clothes help him to get more customers or maybe shock them.

44. WALKING IN THE RAIN

As I descended the steps of the bus, I saw dark clouds in the sky. It looked as though it would rain. I walked briskly towards home which was a few kilometres away. My mother had warned me not to get wet in the rain because I might catch a cold or something. I wondered if I could get home before it rained.

Suddenly, the raindrops started falling down. I wanted to run from the raindrops but my heavy schoolbag discouraged me from doing so. So I walked on.

In a short while I was drenched from head to toes. Instead of feeling miserable, I was actually enjoying it. The feeling of cool water running down my wet body was quite pleasant.

Finally, I reached home. My mother was shocked to see me soaking wet. She hurried me to the hot shower after which I put on clean dry clothes.

She was worried that I might get sick. Well, I did not. In fact, I felt great, having such a wonderful experience of having to walk in the rain.

45. ROAD SAFETY

Everyday many people are involved in road accidents. Some are killed. Many more are injured or maimed. So it is important for us to learn to use the roads properly and safely.

As the roads are very busy nowadays, we should be very careful while crossing it. It is safer to use a pedestrian crossing or an overhead bridge wherever one is available. Never cross a road by dashing across it. It means inviting trouble. In case there are no crossings, then we must look carefully right and left and cross only when it is safe to do so.

It is important that we do not try to get on or off a moving bus. Once I tried to get on a moving bus. It dragged me a short distance and nearly ran over me. I was lucky to escape with only some scratches on my legs. Also, we must not fool around while in the bus. A sudden lurch can send us knocking our heads against something hard.

Using a bicycle can be dangerous, too. We must pay attention on the road and never cycle too far out to the middle of the road. We must obey all traffic rules.

These are some things we can do to avoid accidents. The important thing is to stay alert all times while using the roads. We must know what is happening around us. In that way we can take necessary action to avoid danger whenever we see one.

46. THE HAUNTED HOUSE

Everyone says that the old house at the end of the road is haunted. It used to be the residence of a rich family but now none of them stays there. So the house is vacant and uncared and the compound is filled with over-grown weed and grass.

One evening, me and my friend Varun bravely entered the house and prepared to spend the night there. We brought along a powerful torchlight, two sleeping-bags, some food, drinks, and a portable stereo set. We sat on our sleeping-bags and listened to our favourite music. The darkness was oppressive and there was a strange soft whining noise coming from upstairs.

We were scared and could not dare to go up and investigate about the noise. Varun hurried out of his sleeping-bags and switched on the torchlight.

Suddenly, there was a loud crash from upstairs and the moans turned to screams. We screamed, too, and ran out of the house. The hair on the back of my head stood on end for hours afterwards. After that we never dared to go back into the house, not even in daytime. The next day, my uncle had to go and retrieve the things we had left behind there.

47. THE NEWSPAPERMAN

The newspaperman delivers newspapers to us and many other houses in the neighbourhood. I hear his motorcycle every morning when he comes to deliver the daily paper. He comes promptly at 6.30 a.m. every morning, rain or shine, unless something extraordinary prevents him from doing so.

He is so regular and prompt that I do not need any alarm clock to wake me up. At six-thirty, the neighbours' dogs start barking as he arrives and I know it is almost time to get up for school.

Though he comes every day, I do not get to see him. I only pick up and read the newspaper he had left at the door.

Promptly on the first of each month, at six-thirty in the evening, he shows up with his bills. This time he rings the door bell and I usually have to go and pay him. My mother had got the money ready the day earlier and instructed me to pay him. He is very efficient, very prompt and does not smile even a bit. That is certainly very robot-like.

Nevertheless, I appreciate his reliable service for one thing, that I am never without the daily newspaper. Some of my friends complain that their newspapermen are very unreliable. Not so with mine, he is the best.

48. THE DAY I LOST MY WALLET

When I was seven years old, I was given a small wallet to keep my pocket-money in safely. It made me feel grown up and I carried it proudly in my hip pocket.

One day, during recess in school, I discovered that my wallet was missing. I searched all my pockets but could not find it. I was close to tears. It was not so much because of losing my precious wallet but because I might get a scolding from my parents.

After recess I was in no mood to study at all. I kept thinking about how I lost my wallet and what my parents would do to me. How was I going to explain the loss? I did not know whether someone had pinched it from my pocket or it had merely fallen out. I prayed that someone would find it and return it to me.

Fortunately, I did not have to pay to get on my school bus. My fare was paid for monthly.

When I told my mother about my loss, she was very angry. When my father came home, I received another lecture.

So for the rest of the year and two years following, I carried my pocket-money in my pocket, without having any wallet. I am glad to say I never lost any money again. I had learnt to be more careful and responsible. I had learnt that it is not pleasant to lose something and then get scolded for losing it.

49. CREW CUT

The day I went to school with a crew cut, I was greeted by roars of laughter and plenty of comments. I really looked funny with this hair cut but I was forced to have my hair cut that way.

The monthly ritual of visiting the barber to get my hair cut was tedious. Long hair was like a sin and mine was beginning to cover my ears. My cousin reckoned that he could save me some money if I let him cut my hair. He assured me that he knew how to do it properly. So foolishly I allowed him to use a pair of scissors on my hair. After five minutes of his handiwork, one look in the mirror told me that it was a disaster.

His scissors had created havoc on my beautiful hair! I protested but he assured me that he had not finished and the finished product would be great. The cut was so uneven and haphazard that I had no choice but to visit a real barber to correct the damage. The barber laughed and said that the only remedy was a crew cut. The final result was that my hair looked and felt like bristles, being only two or three millimeters long. At least it looked better than the mess my cousin had made.

I found that a crew cut was not too bad after all. I did not have to comb my hair and my head felt much cooler. As for the laughter and comments, they stopped after a while.

50. MY FIRST ACTING ROLE

The first time I acted in a play was when I was in standard three. I was chosen to play the role of a farmer. Rathi, the prettiest girl in class, played the role of the farmer's wife. So I felt a little elated about my role.

We spent a whole week rehearsing about the play. Learning the lines by heart was tedious. The first rehearsal was a disaster as we fumbled our lines again and again. After half a dozen rehearsals we managed to get things right. It was all very tiring.

The script required me to climb up a mango tree to pluck some mangoes. Obviously, we could not put a mango tree in the classroom. So we improvised by hanging a mango by a string from the ceiling with a ladder below it. Those were the props, placed right in front of the blackboard.

Finally, the day of the play came. I went on stage, rather, in front of the classroom, with my fellow actors and actresses and performed our parts. Everything went smoothly. We never got stage-fright, thanks to our rehearsals and familiar audience of fifteen children.

Now, a few years later, I cannot remember a single line of the play. The only thing I remember clearly is that I enjoyed eating the mango during the play.

51. BIRDS IN MY GARDEN

I live in a bungalow surrounded by a fairly large garden. There are a number of fruit trees growing in the garden along with many plants and a lot of grass. At first glance the garden appears very quiet but actually many birds and animals live in it or visit it frequently.

Every morning I am awakened by the shrill songs of a magpie-robin. The sound is so sweet and I just lie in bed listening to the songs until the bird flies away.

All through the day I see various birds come and perch on the trees and plants. Some come to sing or rest a bit. Others come to look for food. So it is always a pleasure to see them. I just sit quietly and they go about their business undisturbed. I have seen the oriole, spotted-dove, pigeon, yellow-vented bulbul, mynah, fan-tailed flycatcher and various other little birds which I cannot name. They sing, dance and display their beautiful colours. It is quite a treat.

One morning I saw a white-breasted water-hen sunning itself just next to a mango tree. This normally shy bird must really be feeling the pinch of progress to take refuge in my garden.

Some people keep birds in cages to listen to their songs. I say it is far better for the birds to live freely.

52. SOMETHING UNEXPECTED

One morning, we were studying a lesson into the routine when I felt that it was going to be just another day of endless studying. After what seemed a long time, the bell rang for the second period. The Mathematics teacher left. Next would be Geography with Mrs. Paliwal.

The short break between the going of one teacher and the coming of the next was when we had the opportunity to talk and have some fun. It usually lasted a minute or two and sometimes more.

This time no teacher appeared even after five minutes. We were having a great time. Ten minutes – Mrs. Paliwal still did not appear. Our monitor went out in search of her. A few minutes later, he returned to announce that Mrs. Paliwal was absent. We all cheered up. This was unexpected, but it was welcome.

We had great fun. The bell rang again. Forty minutes of fun seemed so short, but it was great while it lasted. Again no teacher appeared. We cheered even louder because it was a double-period which meant we were free till the recess. Altogether we had one hundred and twenty minutes – two hours, of no lesson.

53. A ROBBERY

Sachin helps his uncle to look after the latter's sundry shop. One evening at about 8 p.m., just as Sachin's uncle was about to close for the day, two men on a motorcycle stopped outside. They got off and walked into the shop.

Sachin was about to ask the men what they wanted when both of them drew pistols from their pockets. One pointed a pistol at Sachin and the other at his uncle. Sachin froze and stared at the pistol pointed at him. These two were robbers wearing dark glasses to conceal their identities.

The next moment Sachin and his uncle were made to lie face-down on the floor. Sachin heard the cash register ring and the drawer open. Then he heard a shuffling of feet, the roar of a motorcycle starting up and suddenly all was quiet.

Sachin looked up but the robbers were gone. Sachin shook his uncle who was still prostrate on the floor. Sachin's uncle ran to the cash register. The robbers had taken all the rupees from it. It took less than a minute for the robbers to come and vanish with the day's earning.

Sachin's uncle shook his head. At least the robbers did not harm them. The only thing left to do was to inform the police and let them handle the case. As for Sachin, he learnt to be wary of strangers who wore dark glasses at night.

54. THE IMPORTANCE OF PHYSICAL EXERCISE

Each of us has a physical body made up of muscles, blood, bones and various other living tissues. Exercising the body is one way of keeping it healthy. If we do not exercise then our muscles become weaker and we are less able to do things properly. Also the bones can become weaker and thus break easily.

There are many types of exercises that we may participate in. We may play badminton, football, volley ball or whatever games that we like. We may also jog, walk, or swim. Older folk prefer less strenuous exercises like Tai Chi, Yoga or a leisurely stroll in the park. For the really fit young people, there are rock-climbing, gymnastics and other physically demanding activities.

We exercise to keep our body healthy. However, there are some who overdo things and end up by injuring themselves. It is fine to jog for a few kilometres but it is madness to jog until we are fully exhausted. Also there are people who become addicted to their exercises. They become unhappy when they are unable to exercise or when they lose to someone in a competition.

Exercise is important but neither extreme is good. It is upto us to what extent we should be sensible towards exercising.

55. FREAK WEATHER

One morning when it was still dark, I woke up suddenly. I felt very cold. So I got up and put on some extra clothes. Only then did I manage to get to sleep again.

When dawn came, I woke up to find that my nose was freezing. The rest of the body was comfortably warm under the blanket, but the head, especially the nose, felt like ice.

Anyhow, I got up and immediately felt the cold air around me. I checked the thermometer. It read 19° Celsius. Outside the sky was obscured by thick mist. Again, this was unusual. On my way to school, my clothes actually got damp as moisture settled on me. It was cold and damp. The sun was well hidden. I could not even see where it was.

Most of my schoolmates and the teachers had put on some extra clothes while others shivered.

As the day progressed, it became more pleasant.

Only at about 12 noon did the mist clear and the sun shone through. Even then the atmosphere was pleasantly cool.

It was freak weather, but it was enjoyable while it lasted. It gave me an idea of how it was like in a cold country. How nice it would be if we had this type of weather more often.

56. THE AIR WE BREATHE

The air we breathe is a mixture of many gases, of which oxygen is the most important one. If we are unable to breathe this precious air for even a few minutes, we can die. Thus air is vital to us.

Air is also vital to the plants and animals that live on earth. We are all surrounded by air. Our bodies live and move in it. Thus it is important that the air remains clean and pure.

Alas! modern man has polluted the air. By constantly emitting poisonous gases and fumes into the air from his factories and other devices, man is threatening his own survival.

The air we breathe now is filled with unnecessary and harmful pollutants. If this is allowed to increase then one day we may not have any more clean air to breathe.

So, stop polluting the air. The choice is ours.

57. A BRAVE DEED

Last year, in the month of June, there was a big fire in my neighbourhood shops. The fire brigade took eight hours to extinguish it. The shops gutted were mainly of jute and plastic dealers premises. There were three godowns of plastic toys and two sales depots of jute and gunny bags.

One fireman did the marvellous job there. He was later granted two special increments by the Fire Station Officers for his brave deed. The fire was first reported at about 2.45 a.m. And the fire engines reached the spot at about 3.15 a.m. And everything was reduced to ashes. Luckily, there was no casualty.

The staff of these shops was caught unawares. Two of them fainted due to shocks. It was here that the fireman made them sit, just for two hours, under his care. He was at the first floor, looking after the people in distress. He rendered first-aid to some of the victims of the fire.

He immediately climbed one of the roofs and brought the old man out, with the help of two other workers of the shop. He was praised by the Mayor for his brave deed, and his department granted him two special increments for that.

58. STREET-BEGGARS

Street-beggars are common sight in big cities. Clad in rags, shivering in cold, they could be seen everywhere begging in the name of God. One obvious reason for this evil is illiteracy, poverty and unemployment. There are quite a few who take to begging because of it. But another reason is that begging has become quite a paying profession.

Many evil practices have come into existence because of it. Kids are kidnapped and sold to be trained and used for begging.

They suffer and their oppressors enjoy. Broadly speaking, beggars are of two types – able – bodied and disabled. The able-bodied can work and earn their livelihood, but in the earliest stages they did not get work and now they do not want to work. They find begging easier and more profitable.

The disabled, some due to natural causes and others due to their mentors, have no option. Beggars are great nuisance and are a blot on humanity. They even indulge in many criminal activities. These must be apprehended and taught some craft and made to work. The kidnappers, the sellers and the owners who make the kids beg, should be given exemplary punishments. It is our moral duty to help the weak, hungry and the suffering people. But by dispensing alms as charity, we do not help them. We should help to educate and rehabilitate them.

59. AN UNWELCOME GUEST

A guest is a person to be honoured and respected. But there are certain types of guests who are unwelcome. My father has such an unwelcome guest, named Mr. Lalit. He visits us frequently and always without prior intimation. He knows that my mother is working and we all have to leave at 9.30 a.m.

My father and mother have to go to their offices. We kids have to go to our school. He always comes to our house almost at the time when we are locking up the house or have just finished our breakfast. As he comes, one of us has to stay back and serve him. If mother has casual leave, then she waits.

But mostly I have to stay back as I am the eldest. Then, he is a very easy-going person. He takes his own time in taking bath and getting ready. Mr. Lalit is very fussy about his food. He is not at all considerate. He does not bring his own bedding and we have to supply it at great inconvenience to ourselves. He uses our telephone freely. He not only makes local calls but also trunk calls and does not think necessary to pay for them. He wants my father to take him around in his car and when he goes, he expects father to drop him at the station.

As long as he is there, the whole routine of the house is upset. We thank God when he leaves.

60. MY AIM IN LIFE

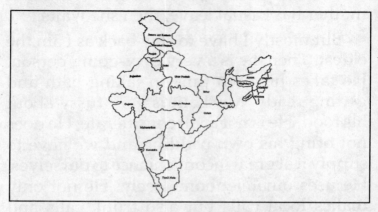

Aimless life is certainly a sin. Different people have different aims in life. Some aim at wealth, some at power, some at fame, some at business and some at education and knowledge. My aim is neither wealth nor fame. I wish to serve my country with the best of my talent. I love India and I really believe that every body should put an effort to make it a great country. I want to become a doctor. It is a noble profession. In medical line, there is much more scope of service.

One can serve the patients everywhere in the country. This is my personal choice. My parents have not compelled me to select it. I wish to become a very successful doctor in future. So I am studying hard to achieve my target. I have keen interest in the medical line, so I do not feel any trouble in studying at all.

After obtaining the medical degree, I plan to work in rural areas where there is much shortage of doctors. My father is a well off man and I do not have any financial problem. I do not have the lust for money. I will visit the rural areas and will help poor people. It would be best sort of service. This will give me extreme satisfaction and that is the aim of my life.

I know, my profession is very dignified and it will help me to get peace and satisfaction in life. It provides one the best chances of service. Sympathy to human being is the sympathy to one's own self.

61. LATECOMING BROTHER

"Is it Jimmy?" "Oh, yes, it is." "Jimmy, you have come home, too very late, is this the time to come home? Answer me, why do you keep mum?"

I shouted on finding my brother Jimmy coming back late, as has been his habit for the past few months. "Shut up! you bloody creature, it is none of your business," saying this Jimmy went to his room and banged the door, adding that he didn't want anything to eat. Thus, ended another of our quarrel, to be precise, heated arguments, and I sinned heavily, as I entered my bedroom. I didn't know why I couldn't get any sleep that night.

Next morning, I woke up, but, with drooping eyes. Nevertheless, I had made up my mind that night, and when Jimmy returned, I sat patiently without uttering a word. When, on feeling uncomfortable of the silence he came to me, I still kept quiet. On further coaxing I started speaking.

I told him how I had once suffered at the hands of my friends, who had betrayed me once they came to know that I had lost my father. I also told him of the time, when my friends had used me for their conveniences. My brother, on hearing this, burst into tears and saying nothing, went to his room.

Next day, when I came back as usual at six, and went inside, I found my brother sitting and studying for his forthcoming examination. Thus ended the truancy of my brother Jimmy.

62. GOOD HEALTH: A BLESSING

Many people don't know that good health brings mental alertness. We should know how to keep ourselves fit and live long. By eating the right food one is able to secure good health. We should develop knowledge about vitamins and minerals in our food and should be aware about the various needs to keep fit.

A famous doctor says, 'Man does not die, but kills himself.' Little by little we kill ourselves by taking wrong food, like sugar, impure water and heavily spiced food, which harm our system and breed diseases.

To bring magic in you, include carrot, onions, garlic and plenty of leafy vegetables in your diet.

It takes more than food to be healthy. Romans and Greeks used to take bath of olive oil, salt water bath and bath of milk and honey for longevity.

Everything in life is as rhythmical as a wave upon wave on the sea shore. To cultivate rhythm, go in the sunshine and take exercise, skipping, jogging, and enjoy vitality and radiant health.

To remain young in spirit, isolate yourself completely and meditate. Meditation makes you incredibly calm and you will never be touchy and irritable. So eat carefully, take exercise for health and cultivate mental energy for a better life.

63. THE MAN WHO INSPIRED ME

Can I ever forget the octogenarian who stayed with us for two days. He was a tall frail-looking man who commanded respect. He had immense patience and strove for perfection in everything. He was sent to stay in our house to avoid the hustle and bustle, the crowd and noise due to a wedding in our neighbour's house. My mother had agreed to have him as she was confident to give him a calm and peaceful atmosphere in our house.

But lo and behold, my sister arrived with her boisterous and rowdy kids for a week. So, my mother had to wake up early in the morning to give milk to the kids before they started screaming. Mr. Rohan the octogenarian was up and mother offered him tea. As she was having tea with him, the kids came crowding in and fired questions after questions.

He calmly sat there answering their questions with such a patience that I was flabbergasted. I would have, by that time been exasperated and brushed them away. They asked him to make one thing after another. He not only made the thing but also strove for perfection. I could not help but ask, why he was taking such pains. It would tire him. Moreover, the children were bound to destroy these things in no time.

He said to me in no uncertain terms, "Young one, never be sloppish. Nothing that has to be done, can be so trivial, as to do it sloppishly. Whatever you undertake to do, put in effort and do it to the best of your ability." Even now when I do something carelessly, his words echo in my ears, He inspired me to take pains in everything I do. I hope I will at least be half a perfectionist as him.

64. HOBBY: A GOOD PASTIME

A hobby is the best form of recreation to mind and body. People's hobbies differ very much according to the character of the person himself. What would appeal to one man might be the subject of ridicule to another.

The best form of recreation is one that can develop in one's awareness, colour, concentration and an observational power. In pursuance of a hobby, one can enjoy one's leisure and learn at the same time.

There are many activities in our life, which can be developed into hobbies or interests. One should choose a hobby wisely. Reading, indoor games, painting, writing, singing, dancing for a boy, or even decorating a house etc. are some well-known hobbies.

Hobbies fill a gap. They can boost our spirit when we are depressed. They makes us creative. Many friendships are formed among people who have common hobbies. The unique quality of a person can be developed with the help of a good hobby.

A hobby eases your mind to be absorbed in something. You have something to show to your friends and something which is educating and brings relaxation to a tired mind. Many hobbies can be used commercially and can bring fame. A hobby is constructive. It gives the mind something positive to hold on to. Nothing can make you feel bored while you have an interesting hobby.

65. A CYCLONE

A cyclone is an area of closed, circular fluid motion rotating in the same direction as the earth. Cyclones are huge revolving storms caused by winds blowing around a central area of low atmospheric pressure.

In the northern hemisphere, cyclones are called hurricanes or typhoons and their winds blow in an anti-clockwise circle. In the southern hemisphere, those tropical storms are known as cyclones whose winds blow in a clockwise circle.

When warm air rises from the seas and condenses into clouds, massive amounts of heat are released. The result of this mixture of heat and moisture is often a collection of thunderstorms, from which a tropical storm can develop.

Cyclones create several dangers for people living around tropical areas. The most destructive force of a cyclone comes from the fierce winds. These winds are strong enough to easily topple fences, sheds, trees, power poles and caravans, while hurling helpless people through the air. Many people are killed when the cyclone's winds cause buildings to collapse and houses to completely blow away.

A cyclone typically churns up the sea, causing giant waves and surges of water known as storm surges. The water of a storm surge rushes inland with deadly power, flooding low-lying coastal areas. The rain from cyclones are also heavy enough to cause serious flooding, especially along river areas.

66. JOURNEY BY BOAT

Once this summer I had an opportunity to go to Mauritius for about a week. We stayed in a hotel which was within walking distance from the sea. On the full moon day, my father hired a boat for two hours. The boat was quite spacious though not a very big one and then I, my father, mother, sister and younger brother clambered in the boat. It was dusk.

The sun had just set. There were not many boats on the river. I wanted to row but my father was afraid to let me do that.

The boatman came to help me and said that he would take care of the boat and mine, too. His words left a trustful impact on my father and thus he agreed.

Then I sat at the place of the boatman and had the joy of rowing for almost ten minutes and course at a lower speed. My brother envied me. Soon the moon was shining brightly. The tall trees silhouetted against the sky made beautiful scenes. The lights of the nearby houses and bridge threw beams of silver in the river.

The sky was studded with stars. The scenery was breathtaking. Time flew, soon the two hours were over. The boatman brought us back to the bank. We enjoyed every single minute that we spent travelling in the boat. It was really wonderful and the memory still haunts me.

67. TRAVELLING BY OVER-CROWDED BUS

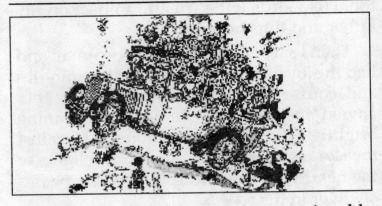

Travelling by bus is an enjoyable experience but I prefer travelling by my car.

Once I was standing at the head of the queue and did not enter as the bus was overcrowded, when a friend came tearing from the rear. She almost forced me to board the bus telling me not to worry as somebody would offer seat to us ladies.

Inside the bus, it was like the plight of the sardine which tries to get out of the tin from its bottom. I had to move from the entrance to the exit to buy my ticket and that too in a bus which was not just packed to the full, but was not even meant for carrying standing passengers.

Twice I found myself in a very uncomfortable position because a co-passenger was trying to relieve his sufferings by smoking. I found myself next to a stinking man. I moved again.

Fortunately, my friend's prediction came true. A young man offered me his seat near the exit. My misery came to an end. I resolved never again to travel by overcrowded bus if I could.

68. THE FUSSY BUS CONDUCTOR

God has created men and women. This conductor, with whom I had the misfortune of travelling, was a fussy one and made the life of passengers miserable whenever he could.

I boarded a slightly overcrowded bus. Some men, women and children crowded near the conductor for tickets. He was shouting at them, particularly at the weaker sections where he expected no retaliation for minor things. Suddenly, he stopped issuing tickets and refused to accept the one rupee note, as it was slightly spoiled. The passenger did not have another note and the fussy conductor was not allowing him to travel without a ticket and finally, asked him to get down. To break the impasse, I exchanged the note. The process of issuing the tickets restarted.

Intermittently, he was almost shouting at the passengers to move forward, to stand erect, as if it was possible, to get into the bus and leave the footboard and threatened to stop the bus, making everyone quite uncomfortable.

Suddenly, he noticed a passenger smoking. He almost pounced on that man and wanted him to throw his cigarette. The passenger was not the one to be easily cowed down. The passengers waiting for tickets, some of whom were nearing their destinations, grew restless and had joined in.

About the same time, the bus reached my stop. I alighted with a prayer that God may give him good sense.

69. A JOURNEY BY CAR

My father bought a new car. We were all very excited. He promised to take us to Agra to visit my grandparents the coming Sunday.

Sunday morning was bright and breezy. We hopped into the brand new car and soon we were heading out of Delhi towards the expressway. My mother sat in the front seat while my father drove. I sat behind with my younger sister.

As it was Sunday, the roads were not very busy. My father is a careful driver and he does not drive too fast. This proved to be good for us because there was a speed-trap manned by the police along the expressway. I saw some cars stopped by the police. Driving along the expressway tends to be monotonous. I actually fell asleep once we passed Mathura.

When I awoke, we were already at the toll gate. My father paid the toll and steered the car towards Agra. My father promised to stop by on our way home. We had to visit our grandparents first.

Finally, we arrived at my grandparents' house in Raja Ki Mandi. The journey had taken about three hours. We stepped out of the car. My grandparents greeted us happily.

70. VISITING A DURIAN ORCHARD

My cousin has a durian orchard about five kilometres from the city. I visited him once during a fruit season.

I reached the orchard at about 9 o'clock in the morning after riding my cycle all the way from my house. My cousin was waiting for me in his modest little wooden house in the middle of the orchard.

Around the house, about 5 acres of it, was the orchard.

There were hundreds of durian trees all over the orchard. Clusters of durians hung on the branches. There must be thousands of these spiny fruits.

Suddenly a loud crash sounded from a distance. I was startled. However, my cousin said that it was only a ripe durian dropping from a tree. Thus I breathed a sigh of relief and followed him to where the sound came from. To my delight I found the fruit among the undergrowth. I picked it up and carried it back to the house.

There were dozens of other durians piled up at the back of the house. My cousin had collected them earlier. They were for a buyer who was coming later. Anyway, my cousin opened a couple of them and I enjoyed eating the delicious flesh inside.

So I spent the morning picking up fallen durians. It was a great time for me. Only the mosquitoes, which kept attacking me, spoiled the fun somewhat.

At about noon time, I bade farewell to my cousin after thanking him for the wonderful experience in the orchard. I then cycled home.

71. VISITING A BOOK FAIR

A Book Fair was being held in the Pragati Maidan. So, one morning our teacher said that we were going to visit there. We cheered loudly with enjoyment because there would be no lessons for the day.

We lined up outside the classroom. Then we marched in pairs to the school gate where our school bus was waiting, Pragati Maidan was just a few kilometres from our school.

At the Pragati Maidan we were told to behave ourselves. If we wanted to buy any book, we were to take it to our teacher. Then we viewed the vast number of books on display there.

It was impossible to look at all of them. So I spent my time browsing mainly among the books on wildlife and nature.

As much as the books were wonderful, the price was discouraging. I could not afford to buy any of them. I would have to ask my mother to buy one for me later on.

Time flew and two hours seemed like two minutes. Soon our teacher told us to assemble at the front door. There she helped those buying books pay at the counter at a special discount. Not many of us bought books as they were too expensive. I did not buy, too. After paying for the books we lined up and went back to school.

72. AT A SHOPPING COMPLEX

My mother and I took the lift from the second level of the underground car-park to get to the ground floor of the shopping complex. The moment we stepped out of the lift, we were greeted by a blast of cool air and the blare of music from a music shop nearby. I could see a goldsmith's shop, two music shops, a pharmacy, two book stalls, a video shop, an optician's shop and a large super-market.

Two very old guards sat in front of the goldsmith's shop. They were nodding off. I wondered if they could cope if robbers were to come to the shop.

A "cheap sale" of clothes was going on in the middle of the foyer. The crowd there was so thick that it was impossible to get near the clothes. We walked past the mad crowd and entered into the supermarket. We picked out the things we wanted and put them in a trolley. When we had finished, I pushed the trolley to the check-out counter where my mother paid for the things we took.

Fortunately, there were few people in the supermarket. The cheap sale had attracted the crowd. So, it did not take us long to buy what we came for. We came out of the supermarket and passed the mad crowd. I noticed that one of the old guards at the goldsmith's was actually snoring! Anyhow, we proceeded to the lift and left the shopping complex.

73. PLACES I LIKE TO VISIT

First of all, I would like to visit the moon. By the time ordinary people can visit the moon, I will probably be very old or dead. Anyhow, it would be quite an experience to walk on the moon. It is said that there is no air and water. I certainly would like to see how high I can jump and how fast I can run on the moon. These are all wishful thinking, of course.

To be realistic, I can only visit places on earth. There are the seven, and other, Wonders of the Earth and I like to visit them all, if possible. After hearing about the marvels of The Pyramids of Egypt, the Great Wall of China, the Taj Mahal, the Leaning Tower of Pisa, the Colosseum of Rome, Stonehenge in England and others, it would be great to actually be there and experience these things first-hand.

However, before all these places, I would like to visit Disneyland first. Which kid would not like to? There are so many things to see and do. It would be great fun.

Right now I cannot visit any of these places. The first reason is the lack of money. The second is. I am too young to go on my own and I do not know anyone rich enough to take me there.

So they remain places I would like to visit. Who knows, I might get to visit some or all of them in future, or not at all. Only time will tell.

74. A VISIT TO THE DENTIST

My tooth hurt through the night. I had to take a painkiller to lessen the pain. Worst of all, I did not get a wink of sleep through the whole night.

The next morning, I told my mother about my toothache. She took me to the dentist. At nine o'clock we waited outside the dentist's clinic. The nurse came and opened the door. She wrote down my particulars and told me to wait a moment. The dentist had not arrived yet. Meanwhile, the tooth still ached like mad.

The burly dentist arrived and I was ushered to the dentist's chair. Normally, I would run away from the frightening surgery with all its horrible drills and pliers, but I did not. So I sat down on the reclining chair while the dentist kept saying some reassuring words. He asked me to open my mouth and I did so. He said that the tooth had to come out and I nodded dumbly in reply.

I felt a slight prick of pain when he gave me an injection, but that was nothing compared to the toothache.

Soon, all pain disappeared. The dentist put a wad of cotton over the wound and he told me to keep my mouth shut for a while. After all, the visit to the dentist was not too bad.

75. A VISIT TO A JUNGLE

A tropical jungle is an awesome place. One day, my uncle Rahim, who works as a forest ranger, took me along on one of his trips into the jungle.

The moment we entered the jungle, a sort of semi-darkness enveloped us. The sky was almost completely shut out by the canopy of leaves high above us. At ground level, thick vegetation grew in every direction. The air was damp and had a peculiar smell to it.

All around us were the sounds of insects, birds and animals. I had no idea how my uncle could find a way through the bushes and trees. As far as I was concerned, I could not see any path.

Nevertheless, I followed my uncle as we trudged along slowly. The most uncomfortable thing about being in the jungle was the leeches. These little bloodsuckers never gave up. Despite thick boots and clothes, they still managed to bite me.

The experience was unforgettable. I was awestruck by the might of nature.

When we emerged from the jungle I felt as though a great weight had been lifted from me. The clear blue sky was a welcome sight. Outside, the world was definitely easier to cope with. The jungle made me feel hemmed in and helpless. It was a good experience but I would never prefer to have a visit to jungle again.

76. WATER SUPPLY DISRUPTION

Disruptions in the water supply do occur now and then. However, there was one that was the worst.

It began one morning when we got up to prepare for the day ahead. All the taps, except one in the bathroom connected to the water tank above the bathroom, were dry. So we had to patiently wait our turn to use the only tap with water.

We did not feel the pinch until evening when the water tank above the bathroom ran dry. My mother had a small tank of water stored in the kitchen, but that was only for cooking purposes. So none of us could have a bath or even wash our hands. Whatever little water we had in various little containers, was used sparingly and we began to be careful not to waste water.

That evening a water-tanker from the waterworks arrived to supply us with water. We ran out gratefully with our buckets to collect as much water as we could. Soon all our buckets were full. At least we could wash ourselves that night.

We carefully used the collected water as we could not afford to waste it.

The next morning, there was still no water from the taps. So again we used the limited water frugally.

Finally, the water supply was restored at about four in the evening. It was wonderful to see rust-coloured water gushing out of the taps. It took a while for the water to become clear. Anyhow, we were glad that we had normal water supply again.

77. HOW I CAN STOP WASTING THINGS IN THE HOUSE

We are lucky to live in a country where we have many things at our convenience. However, we tend to be wasteful.

Electricity is one thing we waste the most. Lights, fans, radios and other appliances are kept on even when no one is using them. I make it a point to switch them off when I do not need them. It takes less than a second to throw a switch but to some people even this seems a difficult task. Anyhow, not wasting electricity reduces the bill appreciably. Thus we do not have to pay for the electricity we do not use.

The other wasted commodity is water. Leaky pipes and faucets plus the negligence of leaving taps running all contribute to this wastage. Fresh water is precious, so it is not to be wasted. It is only a simple matter of shutting off a tap after use. I make sure I do this.

Another big wastage is food. My mother used to cook so much food that much of it was simply thrown away. She knows better now. I pointed out to her about how we wasted food. She realised it and now cooks only what we can eat. The garbage bin used to be filled with half-eaten cakes, fried chicken and things we thought we could eat but could not. It is not so anymore. Besides, we do not waste money on food we throw away.

We waste other things like tissue paper, clothes, soap, talcum powder and aerosol sprays. All these cost money. In short, we waste the money we work so hard to earn.

It is definitely better not to be wasteful. I discover there is a simple method of not wasting things, which is -- use only what we need. Do not touch what we do not need. In this way we can stop being wasteful.

78. TEENAGERS, BEWARE OF THE PITFALLS!

Teenagers today must be ever vigilant to many distractions and dangers that surround them.

First on the list are those distractions that take them away from their studies. Students owe it to themselves and their parents to put in their best efforts in their studies. At all times, therefore, teenagers must make it a point to be conscious of the fact that their studies ought to come first. This strategy will help them get their priorities right. Complete that piece of homework or revise those chapters for the examination before you decide to hang out with your friends.

Next, let's talk about parents. They always have the best interests of their children at heart. However, teenagers often think that parents do not understand them and they are unable to communicate with their parents. If teenagers are a bit more appreciative of their parents and try to put themselves in the shoes of their parents, they will then be able to know how their parents think and feel – of their fears and dreams for their children.

Good friends are always there for you, just like parents. But there are friends who may turn out to be bad influences and can lead you astray. Then there are friends who can inspire you and propel you to achieve great heights.

Being a teenager is not an easy thing. This is the time when there are many temptations and when you grow as a person.

79. DEMOCRACY AND ITS NEEDS

'Democracy,' defines Bernard Shaw, 'is a social order aiming at the greatest available welfare for the whole population and not for a class.' Democracy has many merits. Freedom and equality are its essential concepts. Therefore, there should exist respect for the individual as the supreme motive of power.

Perfect democracy can be achieved by educating all people in a country. People should realise about their social and political responsibilities. They should have a complete knowledge of democratic living and democratic form of government. Constant vigilance is the price of democracy.

The success of democracy largely depends on its power to produce the right type of leadership and things to come are determined by the thinking, value and beliefs of these leaders. They should be conscious about the essence of democracy.

Freedom of expression and a well motivated public opinion through an impartial media will help to achieve effective democratic value. People should be more active and vigilant in the democratic form of government, since it is a government of the people, by the people, and for the people.

Other essences are recognition of the rights of minority, uniform justice through-out the country, citizens to have the right to fight for justice, etc.

Holding free and impartial elections ensures democracy in the true sense. To achieve all these essentials, a basic economic independence of all citizens is a must.

80. HOME LIFE BETTER THAN HOSTEL LIFE

Mohit came home during the Autumn Break for about a week, and met his friends whom he had not been able to meet during the last 2-3 months, as he was staying in the hostel. He was daily surrounded by them, as they were also equally keen to learn from him about his new experiences at the college as well as the playground.

One day one of his friends expressed a wish to be in a hostel, whereupon Mohit had to remark that he was wrong in wishing for the hostel life, and said that their home life was far better than the hostel life. He had various points in support of his belief. These are some of the important arguments put forward by him.

Early in the morning, when one gets up from the bed, one finds father or mother, or some brother, sister or other near and dear one in a home, while in the hostel it is the room-mate or a bearer carrying a tray with cups, full of cold tea being served while one is in bed. You feel like greeting your parents or others, while in a hostel you are terribly annoyed with the servants disturbing your sleep early in the morning.

Then for cleaning, sweeping or for your meals, you have to struggle a lot, as no one appears to be the least bothered about you, or your friends. There, everything is so stereotyped.

In the evening you generally do not get your hot cup of milk, coffee or tea. You have to remind the servant, day in and day out for your share of meals.

One misses the home life most in a hostel, especially on the eve of festivals, as it is not always possible to go home during every vacation, whether it's big or small. The friends and relatives are missed the most.

Whether it is meals or sleep, games or study, cleanliness or comfort, in every aspect home life is better than hostel life.

81. A DAY IN THE LIFE OF A BUS DRIVER

Maniram gets up wearily at 6 o'clock. It is the start of another day ferrying school kids to and from school.

At six-thirty, after a hurried bath, Maniram starts his old mini bus and moves off. He goes along a regular route picking up children to send to various schools. Maniram drives carefully through the busy roads.

He stops at four different schools, dropping off some children at each. He plans his drive carefully so as to reach the last school by seven-thirty. At seven-thirty, his bus is empty and the roads are magically less congested. Most of the children are in the classrooms.

Maniram stops by at a stall to have his breakfast. He comes at eleven-thirty and picks up other school children for the afternoon session. By twelve-thirty he has sent all the children to the schools safely.

At one o'clock he collects his first batch of children from a school. After collecting the children he sends them home.

82. CONVINCING ABOUT STUDIES

Early in the morning my father got up and started calling me. When I woke up, he delivered a full speech, not only on early rising and its good effects on the physique, but also on how to utilise my morning hours for my studies, which he thought, I was not attending to, though I was pretty well almost in all the subjects.

He cited the examples of Rahul and Micky, two of my classmates, who always used to top in the examinations, and were, according to my father, early risers, and very diligent in their studies. According to me, both of them were as ordinary as I was, but luck used to favour them, and they used to get top positions.

I told him that I was attending to my studies as much as I could and he should bless me so that I might also get good marks in the next final examinations. He very reluctantly agreed to spare me as he had to, perhaps, attend to his court duty that day a bit earlier. His senior had called him to the Lawyers Chamber at 8 a.m. that day.

When my father went to the bathroom for a shower bath, I took my bicycle and rushed out. Reaching my friend's house I jumped into his bed and pulling a blanket over me, tried to make good the loss of my slumber which I had to cut short that day.

Returning home, I asked my mother to tell daddy that I was now grown up and responsible, and not to scold me like a child, for I understand and carry out my job very well and they would not worry for me in the next examination results.

83. CONVINCING PARENTS FOR PICNIC

My class was going for an outing, but my parents, especially my father did not agree to allow me to join it. I thought of speaking to him the other day in the evening. The reason was my poor performance in the terminal tests.

First, I made up my mind to be regular in studies. Daily after 8 p.m. I sat for two hours in the drawing room, much in the presence of my father solving sums, while other members of the household enjoying the TV programmes.

My father used to notice it. But no one said anything till a week before the picnic. One day two of my friends dropped in the evening to call me for the evening stroll. I expressed my inability and told them that I could not break my vow to be at my desk for Mathematics at about 8 p.m.

That was the turning point of the drama. My father was now convinced about my studies. He had perhaps a second thought about the whole issue. The day before my departure, he came from his room and asked me to join the picnic, much to the surprise and anguish of all in the family, specially my mother. The need to convince them did not arise because of my care for studies as they were convinced of my actions.

84. CONVINCING A CARELESS LADY

'Madam' I am so sorry to remark that you completely lack the civic sense. Do you realise, in what a miserable plight you have put me? I am going to meet my employer, who has asked me to take up a job in his concern, today. I do not have even time to go and change.

'At least one should have patience, to realise about the consequences, in which one is going to put the other person, by his acts, in which one is absent-mindedly engaged, at a particular moment. You should have kept a garbage tin to store the refuse in your house that you have spoiled my morning. Who would be responsible for my loss, in case I go home in a taxi, for a change of dress?'

The lady felt very sorry at her careless act and came down apologising, and offered to give me a newly pressed suit of her brother, that would fit me properly, or to pay for the taxi charges to go home for a change of suit.

I felt consoled, and after changing my dress, reached my new job on time. This was the beginning of a new friendship.

85. MY PET

I used to have a very special pet. She was a very cute cat. My dad had presented it to me on my birthday. I named her Gucci because she was as cute as the clothes. Gucci was very beautiful.

She had white fluffy fur, one blue eye and the other green, she had a little gray spot on her head, a black spot on her tail, and, had small legs with very cute paws. When my dad gave her to me, she was only three months old; he had brought her from one of his business trips to Russia.

Gucci was a very smart cat; she used to know my timing for every single day. She would wake me up in the morning, a couple of minutes before my alarm clock would sound off, by licking my face. I even cried on the airplane because I missed her so much.

Then, when I opened the door, she would jump on me and start licking my hand as if she was trying to tell me that she missed me so much. I remember that I used to get so happy to know that she was waiting for me. It was a very sad moment for me, I cried with her the whole time while I was packing.

86. OUR ANIMAL FRIENDS

Man is a social animal. This fact itself proves our nearness to the animal kingdom or the animal world. Animals are very faithful and helpful. Right from very early stages a dog is perhaps the only animal who has helped mankind the most.

Next comes the cow. She provides us milk and bullocks for the agriculture work. Horse or the mule is yet another animal who helps mankind in more than one way. A cat is also known to be the best pet.

Children, specially the younger ones, like her very much. They carry her in their arms like a puppy, as she is lighter and softer to handle. Among the animals we can include goats, lambs, hares or rabbits also. The presence of an animal in a house is considered to be a good omen in villages.

Farmers own cows, buffaloes, bullocks, horses, mules, ponies and even asses, for milk, framework and, over and above that, as a status symbol. The animals are our best friends.

87. WHALES

Whales are mammals as are humans, dogs, cats and elephants. They breathe air and so must return to the surface at regular intervals to get a breath. They give birth to live young that stay with the mother for over a year and feed on milk produced by the mother.

Whales are mammals and, therefore, have lungs rather than gills. They decide when to breathe, and come to the surface to do so through a blowhole on the top of their heads. They also surface to breach – lifting their bodies partially out of the water – and slap the water with their tails in impressive displays.

The biggest whale is the blue whale, which grows to be about 94 feet (29 m) long – the height of a 9-story building. These enormous animals eat about 4 tons of tiny krill each day, obtained by filter feeding through baleen. Adult blue whales have no predators except man.

The smallest whale is the dwarf sperm whale which as an adult is only 8.5 feet (2.6 m) long.

Some whales stick their tail out of the water into the air, swing it around, and then slap it on the water's surface; this is called lob-tailing. It makes a very loud sound. The meaning or purpose of lob-tailing is unknown, but may be done as a warning to the rest of the pod of danger.

88. CAMEL

Camel is a large mammal of the desert. It is a cud-chewing animal and has one or two humps on its back. They mature at the age of 17 and live up to 50 years. They are usually dark brown to dusty gray in colour; however, white camels do occur. Camels are often ill-tempered and are known to spit at people, bite, and kick.

Camel is well adapted for life in the desert. It feeds on desert vegetation and can go without water for up to three weeks.

Loaded pack camels can travel for three or four days without water. The secret of the camel's endurance is its ability to conserve water. Its body temperature, unlike that of most mammals, is not constant; instead, it rises during the heat of the day, eliminating the need to sweat or pant and thus conserving water. In addition, little water is excreted in its urine and feces.

The camel has flat, broad feet that enable it to stand on top of sand without sinking. Each foot has two toes with small nails. Tough, horny pads on the feet, chest, thighs, and knees protect the skin from burning when the camel lies down on the sand. Double rows of long, thick eyelashes protect the camel's eyes from glare and sand. The slit-like nostrils can be closed during sand or dust storms. The camel's hump contains fat, which sustains the animal.

89. THE QUTAB MINAR

The tall and ever attractive monument of Delhi which can be seen from many parts of the city, is called the Qutab Minar. It is among the tallest and famous towers in the world. The minaret is 234 feet high and is the highest individual tower in India. It has a number of floors or storeys which has beautiful carvings like the one on the tomb of Iltutmish. There are inscriptions all round the tower and these inscriptions reveal that Iltutmish finished the tower. The structure of the wall is made as such that it widens from top to bottom, just to make the minar stronger.

There are a number of legends related to the Qutub Minar of New Delhi. Some people believe that the monument was actually built by Prithviraj Chauhan, so that his daughter could behold the sacred river Yamuna from its top as part of her daily worship. Since the Qutub Minar's entire architecture seems to be of Islamic origin, these legends seem to be baseless.

However, Hindu craftsmen and sculptured stones of some Hindu temples were certainly employed for its construction, as is evident from the Devanagari inscriptions on its surface. It is said that a cupola surmounted the stone tower originally, which was destroyed by an earthquake. Later, an effort was made to replace it in the 19th century, but it was brought down in 1848. It can still be seen on the lawns to the south-east of Qutab Minar.

90. THE TAJ MAHAL

The Taj Mahal is regarded as one of the seven wonders of the world. The Taj Mahal is the most beautiful monument built by the Mughals, the Muslim rulers of India. The Taj Mahal is built entirely of white marble.

The Taj Mahal was built by the Muslim emperor Shah Jahan in the memory of his dear wife and queen Mumtaz Mahal, at Agra, in India.

The Taj Mahal stands on the bank of river Yamuna, which otherwise serves as a wide moat defending the great Red Fort of Agra, the centre of the Mughal emperors until they moved their capital to Delhi in 1637.

The Taj Mahal rises on a high red sandstone base topped by a huge white marble terrace on which rests the famous dome flanked by four tapering minarets. The garden of Taj Mahal contains a green carpet of grass and a Persian garden runs from the main gateway to the foot of the Taj Mahal.

The purity of the white marble, the exquisite ornamentation, and precious gemstones were used, and its picturesque location, all makes the Taj Mahal a place among the most popular ones. However, unless and until one knows about the love story behind the Taj Mahal of India, it will come up as just a beautiful building. But, the love behind this outstanding monument, is what has given a special life to this monument.

91. DR. RAJENDRA PRASAD

Dr. Rajendra Prasad was born on December 3, 1884. His father's name was Mahadev Sahay and his mother's name was Kamleshwari Devi. Rajendra Prasad was the youngest among his siblings. Mahadev Sahay was a Persian and Sanskrit language scholar.

Dr. Rajendra Prasad was the first President of independent India. He was President of the Constituent Assembly that drafted the Constitution. He was one of the foremost disciples of Gandhiji and played a crucial role in Indian freedom struggle.

At the age of 12, Rajendra Prasad was married to Rajvanshi Devi. Dr. Rajendra Prasad was a brilliant student. He stood first in the entrance examination in the University of Calcutta, and was awarded with a monthly scholarship of Rs. 30. He joined the famous Calcutta Presidency College in 1902. As President he used his moderating influence silently and unobtrusively and set a healthy precedent for others to follow. During his tenure as President he visited many countries on missions of goodwill and sought to establish and nourish new relationships.

In 1962, after 12 years as President, Dr. Rajendra Prasad retired and was subsequently awarded the Bharat Ratna, the nation's highest civilian award. He spent the last few months of his life in retirement at the Sadaqat Ashram in Patna. Dr. Rajendra Prasad died on February 28, 1963.

92. SUBHASH CHANDRA BOSE

Subhash Chandra Bose was born on January 23, 1897 in Cuttack, Orissa. His father Janaki Nath Bose was a famous lawyer and his mother Prabhavati Devi was a religious lady. Subhas Chandra Bose was the ninth child among fourteen siblings. Subhash Chandra Bose was a brilliant student right from the childhood.

Subhash Chandra Bose, affectionately called as Netaji, was one of the most prominent leaders of Indian freedom struggle. Though Mahatma Gandhi and

Jawaharlal Nehru have garnered much of the credit for successful culmination of Indian freedom struggle, the contribution of Subash Chandra Bose has been no less. He has been denied his rightful place in the annals of Indian history. He founded the Indian National Army to overthrow the British Empire from India and came to acquire legendary status among Indian masses.

He passed the Indian Civil Service exam and was elected as Congress President in 1938 and 1939. He formed a new party All India Forward Block, organised Azad Hind Fauj to overthrow the British Empire from India, and was said to have been killed in an air crash over Taiwan on August 18, 1945. But the findings of the Justice Mukherjee Commission disprove it, and indicate that he lived in India as a sadhu till 1985.

93. LAL BAHADUR SHASTRI

Lal Bahadur Shastri was born on October 2, 1904 at Mughalsarai, Uttar Pradesh, and died on January 11, 1966. His parents were Sharada Prasad and Ramdulari Devi. Lal Bahadur's father was a school teacher and later on, he became a clerk in the Revenue Office at Allahabad. Though Sharada Prasad was poor, he lived a life of honesty and integrity. Lal Bahadur lost his father when he was only one and a half years old. Ramdulari Devi raised Lal Bahadur and her two daughters at her father's house.

Lal Bahadur Shastri was the second Prime Minister of independent India. Though diminutive in physical stature, he was a man of great courage and will. He successfully led the country during the 1965 war with Pakistan. To mobilise the support of the country during the war he coined the slogan of "Jai Jawan Jai Kisan".

Lal Bahadur Sastri also played a key role in India's freedom struggle. He led his life with great simplicity and honesty and was a great source of inspiration for all the countrymen. He played a leading role in Indian freedom struggle and became Parliamentary Secretary of Pandit Govind Vallabh Pant, the then Chief Minister of Uttar Pradesh; became the Minister of Police and Transport in Pant's cabinet; appointed as the Railways and Transport Minister in the Central Cabinet; he also held the portfolios of Transport and Communications, Commerce and Industry, and Home in the Central cabinet; and became the Prime Minister of India in 1964, leading India to victory over Pakistan in 1965 war.

Other Books on

WORD POWER SERIES

1. Effective English Comprehension Read Fast, Understand Better ! **(New)** — 150/-
2. Latest Essays for College & Competitive Examinations **(New)** — 150/-
3. Dictionary of New Words **(New)** — 125/-
4. Art of English Conversation Speak English Fluently **(New)** — 125/-
5. Teach Yourself English Grammar & Composition **(New)** — 125/-
6. Common & Uncommon Proverbs **(New)** — 125/-
7. Effective Editing Help Yourself in Becoming a Good Editor **(New)** — 125/-
8. Effective English A Boon for Learners **(New)** — 125/-
9. Essays for Primary Classes — 55/-
10. Essays for Junior Classes — 55/-
11. Essays for Senior Classes — 55/-
12. Dictionary of Synonyms and Antonyms — 125/-
13. Dictionary of Idioms and Phrases — 125/-
14. Common Phrases — 125/-
15. How to Write & Speak Correct English — 125/-
16. Meaningful Quotes — 150/-
17. Punctuation Book — 125/-
18. Top School Essays — 95/-
19. How to Write Business Letters with CD — 250/-
20. Everyday Grammar — 125/-
21. Everyday Conversation — 125/-
22. Letters for All Occasions — 95/-

Unit No. 220, Second Floor, 4735/22,
Prakash Deep Building, Ansari Road, Darya Ganj,
New Delhi - 110002, Ph.: 32903912, 23280047, 09811594448
E-mail: lotus_press@sify.com, www.lotuspress.co.in